SPOKEN FROM THE HEART

DAKIARA

MIND FLOW PUBLISHING & PRODUCTION LLC

SPOKEN FROM THE HEART

By DaKiara

Spoken From The Heart
By DaKiara

First Printing: 2019

ISBN 978-1-951271-00-8 (paperback)

ISBN 978-1-951271-01-5 (ebook)

Additional copies of this book and others are available by mail or by visiting the
website listed below. Check website for pricing.

Mind Flow Publishing & Production LLC

PO Box 48768 Cumberland, North Carolina 28331-8768

www.mindflowpublishingproduction.com

Cover Design by Chy Illustrations

Interior Design by Turbo Kitten Industries

This Book of Poetry is dedicated to all the great Poets that paved the way for me to do what I love.

To my family, thank you for the unconditional support. I know it isn't always easy.

To my husband (Kenny), I love you more than words will ever convey.

To Mesha, thank you but that doesn't begin to say it either. You have been someone who has been with me from the ground up. Even in my crazy moments you continue to stand with me. I've threatened to stop when the going was tough, you kicked me when I needed it.

To my Besties, Meek, Steph, Angie and Marisa, you all have pushed me along to this point. I love you all.

To my friends that I have not mentioned, you are in my heart always and I appreciate you all for contributing to who I am.

SPOKEN FROM THE HEART

From the deepest parts of my heart
Comes these words I write
Maybe they will encourage
Never meant to discourage
Only here to lift up
And speak positives
To help push through the negative
The world is in a state of chaos
But we can unite
And continue to fight
For what is right
Making the world
Safe for all
We are all God's children
No matter the hue of ones' skin
And because of that
We can make the world great again

HEARTLESS

A thousand tears
I've shed
Wondering about
Whose bed
You were lying in
Not to mention
What sin
You have committed
Just because
She said
She was with it
No more
Tears to cry
I know it's wrong
But I wished you'd die
Heartless I know
Definitely time
You have to go

PROMISE

A burden has been lifted
The weight has been shifted
Time to use my talents
That I have been gifted
To show my father
I am grateful
My words
I promise
Won't be wasteful
Instead tasteful
Striving for a great outcome
Praises to God
He is the one
His praises I sing
Blessings he brings

4

HE WON'T WIN

Everyday I'm fighting battles
That only I can win
With the help of my father
For every sin
He forgives me yet again
There is no room
For the devil here
I won't allow him
To feed upon my fear
I know the lord
Has my back
Not being boastful
Just merely stating fact

4

LOLA

Lola was a girl from my class
All the boys wanted
A piece of her ___
Lola was the big flirt
So no one gave a second thought
When she lay covered in dirt
Clothes ripped and tattered
Even her new skirt
Like it didn't matter
People passed her by
Without a second glance
Not knowing she
Just lost her chance
A chance at living
Her body was cold as ice
Nobody thought twice
About her laying there
With all her jewels bear

6

FRIENDS

The true measure of a friend
Is something that can
Only be found within
It's not how many times you cry
But how many tears you've dried
It's not about offering an ear
More about the frustration you actually hear
It's in the way
You add sunshine to their day
Just by being there
When they know
You could be anywhere
It's the feeling of safety in a hug
That's the feeling of true love

6

SISTERS & BROTHERS

Sisters and brothers
Out here struggling
Don't give up
With all you're juggling
Keep making things happen
Even when times are hard
It's worth it to see
Your children playing in the yard
You have come so far
There is no giving up
When you stumble and fall
Remember to hold your head up
While you are down
Remember to pray
That the lord above
Continues to guide your way

SISTERS IN THE STRUGGLE

To all my sisters
I hear your cries
No matter what they say
You will survive
Daily I know you are tested
Raising your babies alone
At times feeling rejected
Know that you are appreciated
Without your guidance
Our youth would be lost
They see your struggle
But even at that cost
You hold on
And boys become men
Girls become ladies
In the end
So your struggle is not in vain
Keep pushing through the pain
Your tears are symbolized
By the rain

Hold strong
You are not alone

YESTERDAY

Sitting back
Reflecting upon my thoughts of yesterday
Children of different hues
Would laugh and play
I remember chasing
The ice cream truck
Back in the day
And not worrying
About what others
Had to say
Some say ignorance is bliss
But still those times I miss
My friends were my friends
No rules we would bend
In our own little world
Happy to be
Just boys and girls

FIGHT NIGHT

Almost every night
For the past year
I was guaranteed a fight
Constantly living in fear
In my mind
I knew it wasn't right
Late nights
Of stumbling in
Only satisfaction for you
Was knowing you left your mark
Upon my body
Knowing that nobody
Would look twice
Thinking back
That wasn't very nice
A punching bag for you to use
Patiently awaiting your abuse
When does this cycle end?
Perhaps then my heart will mend

MY FIRST LOVE

As I hear
Your first cry
I ask myself
Why
I wasn't ready
I wasn't prepared
More than anything
I can't lie
I was scared
To be a parent
In this day and time
Patience, I know
I must find
Your smile eased
My worries
I promise
I felt the flurries
In my heart
The two of us together
Never apart

WRITING JONES

When the pen begins
To glide across the paper
I know it's time
To vibe again
All four corners
Of my mind
Begin to speak at once
Each over talking the next
Instead of patiently waiting
I'm eager to see
What's released next?
Will it be about love?
Or life
Hardships & strife
As the words begin to flow
My mind is thinking
Of some more
Several hours later
The pen is still gliding
The cycle continues
I'm caught up in the rapture

DAKIARA

13

SHATTERED GLASS

5 dead
Is what the paper read
A family slaughtered
In cold blood
Just because
Their car
They wouldn't give up
A 02 Malibu
Nothing fancy
Not high class
Shots rang out
"Shattered glass"
The mom shouted
5 limp bodies
On the curb
For a car
Not worth a dub

14

DAYDREAMS

Never one for cheap thrills
Looking for the long term
Netflix and chill
You know the sitting on the porch
About to get scorched
From the sun beams
Just a dream,
It seems
I see us as clear as day
Your smile
Forever to guide my way
Like the beat of the drum
I know I found the one

FOREVER GRATEFUL

You walked into my life
Now I am unable to imagine
My life before you
Became my wife
Loving me is never easy
But you continue to stay
Keeping me centered
Your smile lighting my way
Forever grateful
Even when you are hateful
It still flutters my heart
To know that it's till death do us part

WATCHING ME

Watching you
Watching me
How is this love
Meant to be
You came into my world
Fiercely proclaiming
I was your girl
A proclamation
Even I couldn't deny
As time went by
It was easy to see
Why you were my guy

REMEMBER

Looking back over the years
We've had more than
Our share of ups and downs
Still we persevered
There was the time
I fell out of love
Not with just you
But of this life we share
Thankfully you continued
Holding on
And I remembered
How we got there
A moment of insanity
Is not that rare
To bring me back
You only had to stare
At me with those
Brown eyes
And that mischievous grin
The devil in disguise
Has done it yet again

SIMPLE THINGS

Sitting here
Caught in a daze
Trying hard
To remember
The simple way
You would call
My name
I could always
Hear the smile
In your voice
It warmed
My heart
Knowing
I was your choice
Now I'm left
With memories
Of days past
One day
Together again
At long last

BY MY SIDE

This is the 1st day
Without you by my side
I thought it would be easy
As the day drifted by
My eyes begin to fill
At the thought
Of you not being here
How do I go on?
Pushing forward
Trying to weather this storm
When all I want,
You by my side

MOMENT

In a moment life changed
In an instant my world rearranged
Feelings all over the place
From the simple smile upon your face
Your eyes dance
Holding me in a trance
Out of the blue
I kissed you
From that moment, I knew
I loved you

FOREVER

You said you want forever
Only if you promise to never
Abandon the love
That is constantly growing
From the seeds
We've been sowing
Forever is a long time
No playing games
With each other's mind
This love, I will try to protect
If one crosses the line
I will be quick to correct
This love is true
But truthfully
It came out of the blue
Forever, I cherish you

HEARTBEAT

My heartbeat races
From the thought of you
My soul yearns
When you are away
With each beat
My love for you grows
I love you from your head
Down to the tips of your toes
I feel you deep within my soul
Laying my head upon your chest
The rhythm of your drum
Is my sweet lullaby

IF YOU WANT MY HEART

If you want my heart
You must put in work
It's very intricate
With many working parts
To love me is an art
Many have attempted
But the journey was harsh
So gave up they did
Somehow you have persevered
My heart has been captured

STOLEN GLANCES 2

Stolen glances
Taking chances
Some teasing
Definite pleasing
Random thoughts
Feelings fought
But love wins
Yet again

TEMPTATION

Temptation is a beast
Can it be tamed?
Or is it better left unleashed
It can feel like a drug
And have you strung out
Tweaking and such
When temptation calls
Will your will win out
Or will you simply bend
To temptations whim

TENDER KISS

When your lips touch mine
It takes me to a place
That was once hard to find
Somehow you invaded my space
You encouraged my grind
Just from the look on your face
I see how proud you are
We've come so far
Your tender kiss
Is what I miss
I try to drink you in
And it starts again

THE DATE

My day started with promise
A simple 5 minute call
Several rings went by
Then you answered
With a hi
From there a plan was made
Throughout the day
I ran different scenarios
Thinking what I would say
The truth is
It didn't go that way
I smiled, you smiled
The talks began
We disagreed
And before long
You were giggling
Your eyes danced
My eyes entranced
I could feel my heart
The pace quickened

DAKIARA

I felt a flutter
As our hands touched
That moment
I realized just how much
I needed this date

DEEP

When we met
Truthfully I didn't know what to expect
I knew we would vibe and connect
Somewhere along the lines
My heart interjected
You touched me in a place
My sacred space
Where not too many venture
And gently wrote your signature
Had me wondering if this feeling
I will keep
What can I say?
Your touch is deep

SOFT WHISPER

A gentle breeze
Passes by my ear
Feels like a soft whisper
As my eye begins to tear
I can smell your scent
From the last days we spent
Into my life you were heaven sent
Just as quickly as you entered
All my thoughts became centered
Around you
The love was new
As quickly as you came
The love was taken away
I woke to a new day
One without you
A gentle breeze
Passes by my ear
Blowing away my fear
To continue without you

ALL FOR YOU

You have a style all your own
Doesn't matter if you are in a
Crowd or all alone
Calm cool and collected
Your touch electric
Your skin sun kissed
Smile can't be dismissed
Heart of gold
Feelings turned bold
A few stolen stares
A love rare
The gods blush
As my feelings begin to rush
A love destined to be true
My love all for you

FLAWS AND ALL

I saw you walking by
I smiled to myself
Thinking my, my, my
You are just so fly
When your eyes met mine
I stopped in my tracks
It was only a matter of time
Until you blew my mind
All your sweet talks
While holding hands
For our night time walks
On the beach, or down by the park
You loved me, flaws and all
As time passed by
I was destined to fall
For you flaws an all

HEY PRETTY GIRL

Hey pretty girl
Inside and out
Don't let someone
Make you self-doubt
Look in the mirror
It couldn't be clearer
You are a beautiful being
It's not your fault
If they can't see it
There is no perfect 10
But then again
Just know you are perfectly you
You are in the chosen few
Stays focused and see through
Those who try to shame
For them it's just a game
In the end you will win
See the beauty within

TOOTIE

When I see you
I see the strength
Of more than a few
It is amazing
Seeing God
Through your view
I see the courage
To continue pushing through
When times are rough
You stand your ground
Showing just how tough
Your faith can be
You have prayed for us all
Keeping us from stumbling
Destined to fall
Today we celebrate you
And your faith
Which has been tried?
But remains true
Long story short

We simply love you
You gave us an excellent model
That forever we will follow
Today and all days where you lead
We will follow

BECAUSE OF YOU

Because of you
I took a chance on love
You came through
Taking my heart
With you
From day one
I simply knew
You were my equal
My soulmate even
I often feel as if I'm dreaming
When I'm in your arms
I feel safe from harm
If this love is meant to be
From others I will flee
Loving only you

LOVE

Love is many things
It can be euphoric
And keep you on an emotional high
It can be stifling
And make you wish to die
Love is pleasure
Love is pain
Only the truest of loves will sustain
The trials and tribulations that life puts before you
Honestly what would you do?
Would you stay?
Would you run?
And take a chance that the pain
Will be undone

I LOVE YOU

To say I love you
Doesn't begin to express
My feelings for you
Your touch and caress
Excites my flesh
You challenge me
On a deeper level
With you I feel free
I know that you are on my level
Wishing you could see
The true me
Your smile is etched in my mind
I know that within times
Your heart will be mind
I love you
From the deepest parts of my soul
Take my hand to have and hold
When god made you
He truly broke the mold
You are one of a kind

Smiling to myself
And all mine

YOUR KISS

Sitting here listening to the rain
Thinking about all the pain
I've gone through
Because of you
We fuss
We fight
At the end of the night
Enveloped within your arms
Snug and tight
I daydream of your kiss
How I truly miss
When you aren't around
To keep me on solid ground
I'm aware
Just how much you care
But that kiss
Is what I miss

DEDICATION #1

My heart weeps
Just when I thought
You were mine to keep
It seems as if
You were snatched away
My heart will forever mourn
You the first born
Though our time seemed brief
I sigh, a breath of relief
God knew what was best
We forever will be blessed
You touched us all
In so many ways
To our heavenly father
I pray
He keeps you close
Because in the end
I know he loved you most.

DEDICATION TO REV

You built a foundation
Of hard work and growth
My tribute to you
Is doing the most
I will continue
To carry the torch
To help guide their way
Showing them daily
Christ is the way
The truth and the light
And they must always
Try their best to do what's right
Following in your footsteps
Walking the path
So not to face
His wrath
You were the architect
Truthful fact
And we are so thankful
For that
The lives you touched

The numbers too much
The souls you helped save
That debt never to be repaid
You were a servant of god
And for many years
We did this thing called life
Together
Hand in hand
I know without a doubt
You are watching over me
With every breath I take
Each step I make
You are with me
And your soul
Is finally free

WHEN I LOOK AT YOU

When I look at you
I see you as our king
On this day we honor you
You have proven your love
Through and through
You are our provider
You are our source of strength
Yet, on the inside you are my teddy bear
You can be fierce
Yet, so soft
You wear so many hats and never complain
You just carry it in stride
For that alone
I am happy to be by your side

DEAREST DAD

I wanted this birthday to be
Second to none
I wanted you to know
That you are the one
Who brings joy into my day,
So in my own special way
I wanted to say
You are the sun that brightens my day
For that I can never repay
All that you have brought into my world
And I love being daddy's little girl
No one can ever take your place
You make it look easy
When it comes to pleasing me
You are an amazing dad
It makes me glad
Happy Birthday to the World's Greatest Dad

42

AS I WATCH

As I watch you with our children
I am in awe
How does a man of such strength;
Show such tenderness
You are our king
Of this there is no doubt
You have proven time and time again
To the end of the earth
You would go
I wonder just what traits they will get from you
They follow you as if mesmerized
I should know, I've been mesmerized too
You can be fierce
Yet, soft
You wear many hats but refuse to complain
You simply carry it in stride
Happy birthday to a wonderful father and my best friend

HOW MANY OF YOU

How many of you
Have had to watch as you're loved
One went through
The changes of life
You know where they regress instead of progress
Those once full of life
Now seem to struggle to thrive
Just to stay alive
For those who endure this everyday
My heart aches with so much to say
Sometimes words are never enough
Just know that I understand your
Journey is indeed tough
Most of you would never say it
Or never feel it is a subject to be debated
God has simply called you for a task
This small thing has been asked
For this your place has been secured
Your unconditional love has endured
You have a heart of gold
And your story for many years will be told

MY LOVE

Over the years
I've seen you grow
Into a man
Whose pride is reflected
In his love for his family
You have given
So much of yourself
To countless others
Asking for nothing in return
The more you give
The more they take
But, it's not enough
To make you forsake
Those in need
Of your many kind deeds
You are an amazing
Mentor and father
Who puts family above,
All else
The many lessons

You've taught
Will live on forever

LOST

Starring into your pretty browns
I get lost
Through them I see the universe
Constantly changing
Remaking itself
Into what we need the most
Your smile is wide as the pacific
At times
I feel as if I'm drowning
Your arms are
My own floating device
Always there to pull me up
When life tries to pull me down

TODAY

Today is the day
That I take my life back
I've been beat down
Talked about
To where I began
To doubt myself
And question my worth
My rightful place
In this world
That I tried so hard
To conform too
For so long
I worried how others felt
That I forgot
To pay attention
To how I felt
Today I realize
My life matters
Today I reclaim
My rightful place
Upon my thrown

AS WE LAY 2

Watching you as you sleep
A small smile
To your face it creeps
Wondering, what you're thinking
Are you possibly dreaming?
Knowing you as I do
You are just scheming
On cue
You roll over
Pulling me in for a snuggle
Tonight's a good night
The covers, no struggle
No worries
Of the things
We never say
I am content
As we lay

FOR KEEPS

When I close my eyes
Instantly thoughts of you
Take over my mind
I realize
True love never dies
You've got me
Under your spell
A place I know
All to know
I wonder
If it's me you see
As you sleep
I know
In my heart
This love is for keeps
Bounds I would leap
To ensure
Your love I keep

IN MY OWN WORDS

I seem to get tongue tied
When I express my thoughts
Or the thoughts
I saw on a card
So I decided to open up
And tell you
Just how I feel
In my own words
If that's ok

You have me
On a natural high
Your love has me chained
For you I will gladly remain
My heart flutters
At just the thought of you
My body reacts
As if you used voodoo
Being around you is euphoric

I can't ignore it
You are the sun
To my moon
The fork
To my spoon
The brown
To my sugar
Without you
I'm too through

50

FRIENDS TO FAMILY

When the introduction was made
The connection was fine
Wasn't quite sure if it would fade
Or stand the test of time
We laughed and cried
Pushing through the hard times
But no matter how they tried
Losing this friendship would be the true crime
You became an auntie
As did I
The families were bonded
No need to lie
A bond we promised to never break
No matter how long it takes
We saw through the fakes
Now a bond to strong
To be undone
In the end, we both have won
Your struggles became mine
And for me that is just fine

You've held me up
When I wanted to give up
When friends become family
Everyone wins

51

WRITING FUN

Sitting in my zone
The words begin to fill my dome
What will todays verse bring
What song will the words from my heart sing;
As the words form
I bring forth the first poem
Then escapes another
This one about a young mother
The next about a brother
Who during a fight, his wife smothered
With no second thought
The next was brought
This one came to teach
The youth of today, I must reach
This is a battle that can be won
As the words pour
I'm having some fun

SERPENT

Like a vulture
Watching its' prey
I can feel the evil
And I can't allow it to stay
Your presence doesn't intimidate me
In the way you pictured it
My faith is much
Stronger than you knew
The more jobs you take
The stronger you make me
In the end
You really should thank me
For all the good I've done
But instead you thought
You've won

HELPING HAND

My heart reaches out
To those in need
Whether it's money
Or simply a kind deed
Although I'm not perfect
My soul strives to be
So when I reach the gates
My soul will fly free
If you are kind to others
You will never have to wonder
Or doubt
What you are truly about

INSPIRATION

When inspiration hits
I can feel the tingle in my spine
I know, it's my time
I've pushed through the pain
I'm now dancing in the rain
Of my tears
No longer restricted by my fears
There is no limit
To the words I will emit
I must admit
I'm nothing without you
It's a beautiful thing
When inspiration hits

APPRECIATED

I know I don't say this often enough
But, you are appreciated
More than you know
Without you pushing me forward
I wouldn't have had the courage
To pursue this dream
Writing and making this cream
I know I may ask a lot
It just helps to thicken the plot
Of this thing we call life
You have kept me straight
You never seem to hesitate
That I truly appreciate

DEDICATION #3

Stepping into the new you
Can be a little frightening
Take a little time, to get to know you
And then, walk out with purpose
You have already done your family justice
We are here to give you a nudge or two
Trust me love, we aren't judging you
The path you take is yours alone
Always know you can come back home
In times of confusion
Don't be tricked by the illusion
You are awesome
And in your own way, have taught us
That when times get rough
We must rise up and be tough
You were the first to graduate
My apologizes for not being there
In person to congratulate
Words can never express how my heart feels
Know that I am with you still

Forever and always
Eternity plus two days

Auntie Loves You

BLACK MAN

As a black man
You are thought inferior
Constantly blamed
Not to mention shamed
No hoodies
Or bandanas for you
Quick to put you into a crew
Or worst yet, throw you away
When they are through
Using you for your brain
Then portray you as dumb and lazy
Truth is, those who underestimate you
Are crazy
You've built skyscrapers and empires
Your passion I most admire
Even after being tossed into the fire
From the fire diamonds are formed
Watch out
A black man has been born

AFTERWORD

Thank you for taking the time to read my words. They are truly from the heart. I love people of all hues and shapes. I hope that my words will touch you in the way they are meant to be received. Many Blessings to all.

ABOUT THE AUTHOR

Although still considered new to the Publishing world, I have hit the ground running full speed ahead. In my first year, I was signed to Mind Flow Publishing & Production LLC, and I have published a total of 6 books. I have earned Amazon's Best Sellers Top 100 orange banner. My works are spread across several genres such as; poetry, inspirational, and Christian fiction. I will be trying my hand at cozy mysteries, romance, and sci-fi. My love for writing started when I was about 12, writing poetry and writing speeches for oratorical contest. Inspiration for my craft is pulled from my own life experiences, as well as others. I have been featured on several podcast, as well as Up and Coming Authors Newsletters. When I'm not writing, I love to design shadowboxes, and create personalized greeting cards. I will be releasing my 3rd poetry book (Spoken from the Heart) and a minimum of 2 novellas (Charisma's Homecoming, For Her Love) before the end of 2019. Current books available are The Mary B Chronicles 1 & 2, Mental Interlude, and Journey to Living, Simple Complexity, and Dreams Do Come True. All of which are available on Amazon, and www. mindflowpubpro.com.

www.ingramcontent.com/pod-product-compliance
Lightning Source LLC
Chambersburg PA
CBHW060350050426
42449CB00011B/2906